# Enlightenment

# in a café

## Spiritual comfort with a cup of coffee

### A. R. Matkins

The door to our inner being can never be truly shut, because there is always love ready to open it.

# INTRODUCTION

How wonderful it is to sip a cup of good coffee in your favourite café, to find that peaceful moment when you can be with yourself regardless of the conversations that might be going on around you – finding a space that is your own.

In solitary moments like these I will sometime just gaze out through the café window to the world outside; other times I will write down my thoughts. These are usually a reflection of what is going on for me, what is inside of me that needs to be either remembered or recorded, or just how I am feeling that day. There have been moments when, inexplicably, I am caught in another space and the words that flow onto the pages of my small notebook are not any that have entered my thoughts; my thoughts have been put to one side as other voices have added their own. In those moments I have to read what I have written when I put down the pen, read, and absorb words that show me another view of life, another view of what can happen in our imaginings.

But is this just imagination, or are we all capable of tuning into something that is outside of our physical vision but nonetheless has a link to us, and above all wants to communicate? These communications can sometimes come at times of great need, and when they do I find I return to them again and again and discover that what is said has love written into every sentence and every page.

Language can have many layers of meaning, which is why my spirit friends impressed on me the need to *not* change or edit anything I was given. It was important for their words to be left open to personal interpretation by whoever read them. It was not for me to meddle. I could, of course, meddle all I liked with my own jottings as they were all my own words.

I trust that whoever reads this little book may find something that reflects what you have felt or experienced for yourselves. Perhaps you guidance is saying much the same, but with different words?

Go well . . .

A. R. Matkins

~

April 2021 - As I write, the U.K. is just coming out of another Lockdown. My wish for you all is that you will continue to enjoy many more café moments of your own.

# PART ONE

# THE MESSAGES

The messages that follow are from different sources; different Beings. Some have preferred to remain anonymous, while others have chosen only to refer to themselves as "Messengers".

One, who is definitely not anonymous, is Pierre. And, yes, he is French! Pierre is someone who came into my life many decades ago – a gentle soul, with a strong sense of who he is, but always prepared to say what needed to be said. He has experienced many incarnations on earth, some of which have been as a free-loving, free-living being, as well as a cloistered one. He understands what it is to be human!

*When the sun has gone to bed and the moon is in the hills, reach out and touch the sky.*

*Let the heavens open to your sight, revealing wonders beyond your comprehension.*

~

Manifest good thoughts

every day.

They will rebound on you in the same

way that bad thoughts do.

But with a far better outcome.

~

*When you look at life you see that it has a rippling effect, coursing to and fro, round and round.*

*As energy flows and ebbs it takes time, even after the last flow, for the last eddy to die down. Within, you still ache; without, you are stiff and tense. But in your heart and spirit the endless ebb and flow of emotion is coming to a stop.*

*Let things take their natural course, go with, not against, the flow.*

*And don't be a doormat! Ever!*

*. . . Pierre*

~

"Out of time"

is a timeless zone

where you see the world

differently.

And, maybe,

as it should be seen.

~

*Do not look for the downside to current global thought. Lift people up over the hurdle that governs their excessive need to feel that they are "hated". Hated is a strong word, but if they cannot believe they are loved then what other alternative do they understand?*

*Tread carefully over people's feelings. Give them your ear, but not your heart. Keep that quiet and intact, at peace and resonating with goodness.*

*See the wonder in everything rather than looking around its edges for the shadows. Shadows there will always be, but that means there is also light.*

*So, be uplifted into Higher Consciousness, and give thanks.*

*And don't get political.*

*. . . Pierre*

~

when there are thoughts of

regret,

wipe them clean

with what you can do

about it.

~

*You are what you are and there's no need to deny it. If a decision needs to be made and you make it feeling the rightness of it then you are, of course, following your true instincts.*

*A false trust is not the way. To pretend to accede to another's wishes is a lie to the universe. Be honest. Truth does not hurt. It only hurts when it is not the truth we want to hear.*

*All will be well. Valuable lessons are hard, difficult, but necessary. "Let sleeping dogs lie" is a favoured saying, but moving energy towards a compromise is only favoured when both sides feel happy and content with the outcome. More often than not people are never happy even when wishes are granted. For, like prayers, they are answered differently from how we would wish.*

*Peace in the heart, and good wishes too, will heal the process.*

*. . . Pierre*

~

Repose is a sweet nothingness

that we all

wish for ourselves.

~

*Animals have sense, feeling and love. They may not be able to voice an opinion, but that doesn't mean to say they are dumb.*

*Look into their eyes and see the intelligence there, and also the understanding. Look into their eyes and say, 'I love you'.*

~

Choose your words

carefully.

For the universe

hears them.

~

*When casualness becomes laziness, then you must be aware that it is only you who is going to come and tidy up your spiritual life for you.*

*Nobody else.*

~

Playing games should be

fun, uncompetitive and ecstatic,

in the joy of human

movement.

~

*What is the most important thing to strive for? Perfection in this life or the next?*

*Nothing that is of the material is perfect. Have what you deem lends beauty and character to your life, for all things are in the eye of the beholder. And what does it matter if it is only you who sees it?*

~

Memories are hopefully fond.

But if there be sadness,

cast a thought to the world.

And what your sadness

adds to.

~

*The mystery of life flows ever outwards, but now and again there is an inner chord that hums and sings to its owner of things other than that which lives in physical reality.*

*Unconscious desire vibrates and renews our tissues, our blood, and forces renewed energy into our being so that we resonate with life-giving forces that heal and re-form and re-connect (even removing disease), in the wondrous way that atoms and molecules react to this loving force.*

~

Imponderables

should stay

where you put them.

~

Although this is a message for me, you might know how this feels, too:

*You fret about a lack of talent when all it is, is not having those skills you wish to have, whilst not admitting to those skills you do have. It is not a contest, this life. It is about using those abilities that are inherent in you for this lifetime until they are fine-tuned, honed to as near perfection as can be.*

*Contentment is a definitive virtue. It is not smugness, nor is it lassitude: it is a feeling of being at peace with your world whatever part of it you are dealing with at present.*

*Seek to do the best you can do with whatever you have, and always with good intent.*

*. . . Pierre*

~

We are all conscious beings.

You just haven't

woken up to it yet.

~

*In the midst of wakefulness there is an eternity of mind where thoughts dwell in easy company with peace, calmfulness, and a feeling of utter contentment.*

*To touch this we must relinquish all desire, all need to know what is or what is not. Keep only that moment in your heart as a pulsing rhythm of perfection, a living moment that nurtures.*

*There is no one moment that is better than another. Each moment is a breath, a touch of something to which we belong and yet seems unfathomable. But there is no real need to fathom, only to be conscious of how the self is revealed in that moment.*

*. . . a Messenger*

~

Nuisances are casual affairs,

which is why it is best

not to pay them

any

attention.

~

*There is much to be said for clever minds and intellectual, academic minds. They help to shape our world.*

*It is to be hoped their cleverness and wisdom can also accept the jokiness of the world.*

~

His spirit

is with you.

The Holy One.

~

In the Psalms of the Bible there are paeans of joy and light.

But each of us can sing our joy, and we are all able to have a direct contact with a God that can also sing and join with us in joy.

*. . . a Messenger*

~

Try to do something you don't like.

It will help you understand

why others don't like it

either.

~

*Conflict. Is there anything good to say about it?*

*Only, that when resolution comes, it is the sweetest of soul healings if the resolution is accompanied by love.*

*. . . a Messenger*

~

All that pertains to good,

can only be good.

For it comes from goodness.

~

*There are many ways to say 'hello' and 'goodbye'.*

*If said from the heart, then the other's heart will respond to the 'hello' in like manner, and the manner of the said 'goodbye' will be remembered, and taken with the one it is addressed to.*

*So be sure that your words come from your heart, and pay attention to the feelings they convey.*

*. . . Pierre*

~

Our little idiosyncrasies blur

the perfect picture

that is our

true selves.

~

*A flower is a flower, is a flower.*

*A wood is a wood, is a wood.*

*So different, but equally beautiful.*

*As everyone is.*

~

Freewill is

a gift.

Don't

misuse it.

~

*Families are important. They are the glue that seals the cracks in our lives, filling those cracks with love and laughter.*

*That is how it should be for all of us, but then we are not all the same or all on the same track in our soul's evolution. There can be moments when we question our connection to our family, why we might feel they are different from us. Are we in the right family? Has someone got it wrong and our family are not the ones we've chosen?*

*Oh yes, chosen. This is an indisputable irony that we choose our parents, our siblings, our relations, for they are the pre-determinedners as to how our life will unfold. They are the signposts, the crossroads; the traffic lights along our road to knowing who we are.*

*Have faith in the blessing of your family. Understand how it is for them to have you as part of their lives, and how love shared can cure all ills, overcome all unwillingness to be as they are. Take from your family the wisdom of knowing each other as outsiders will not ever know you.*

*. . . Pierre*

~

Do not be troubled

about accidents.

They are the universe's

Way of getting you

To pay attention.

~

*When doubt assails you, lift your heart to the heavens and be assured that there, there is perfect symmetry and harmony. Doubt has no room in the order of things. To be doubtful is to deny this order. It is to put yourself out of reach of the cosmic harmony.*

*When in need of confirmation, hold the thought within and quietly allow it to penetrate. How does it feel? Comfortable? If not, release the thought and wait; wait until that which is sure and positive comes through.*

*Do not argue with yourself. No matter what the pressure, do not jump to another's tune. Live within each moment as if it were perfect and whole in every respect.*

*Even so-called mistakes aren't so. They are just a pointer to finding true answers.*

*. . . Pierre.*

~

'Come ye all who are

heavy laden

and I will refresh you.'

This is the call of the

spirit

to your weary heart.

~

*The mind of God is an All-seeing, All-enveloping mystical mask of creation.*

*What you understand in your everyday experience is the minutiae of the cosmos. Your particular piece of the cosmic order is nonetheless precious and valued. It is an intrinsic part of the harmony of universes, the stretch and pull of a living entity that knows all things, is all things, and encompasses all things.*

*You see the swirling whirling galaxies hanging in a dark cosmic void and wonder at the immensity of it all. What holds it all together even? Do planets, stars, galaxies know their course? Do they set their own course? Or are they creatures of habit; once they revolve they keep revolving, knowing no other way to be and not particularly caring, because part of the knowing compared with the "not knowing" is that they fit with perfect symmetry into the WHOLE?*

*Man searches for meaning in his small world, when actually the meaning is embedded in every cell of his physical being.*

*You reach for patterns in the sky when there seems to be randomness, but it is a chaos that has form and intent.*

*It lives in a natural order.*

~

All is good

All is God.

~

*The substance of life is but a simple matter of knowing beyond trust. Trust is a fine word and is imagined as a brother to faith. But knowledge far outweighs both of these.*

*Wisdom is what all seek, yet it cannot come from anywhere else except knowledge. But true wisdom must also come from love, from understanding what it is to care for others and to know thyself with love. It is not enough to love others and the world if you do not love yourself – to whatever degree – less or more, or somewhere in between.*

*When you have love of this kind, and knowledge, then you will have wisdom, a wisdom that seeks only to be a partner to peace and calmfulness. That, like the still lake, is never ruffled.*

*But also never be arrogant. True wisdom is modest, seeking neither merit nor reward.*

~

Courtesy is a dying art.

And yet it costs nothing

to cultivate it.

~

*Heed not the friendly warnings of others, for their task is different from your own.*

*Rather, reflect within for that calm, quiet space that brings you home. Home to your roots, your ineffable being; your fathomless seed of divinity.*

*Then act.*

~

Harm,

harms the harmer.

That is universal law.

~

*Do not be captured by false imaginings. Test what you don't know.*

*How does it feel in your heart?*

~

An overview of one's life is an

overview of oneself.

~

*For as often as you can, link to your connection with the universe – to see your link, your attachment, with loving eyes and heart. Then it will always serve you in infinite wisdom.*

*Your creed is: 'Here I am!'*

*There comes a time when you have to confront life, life as you know it. Change is about refreshment, a coming home to what no longer serves you, what can be allowed to be released, leaving space for the new and more vibrant.*

*. . . Pierre.*

~

Knowledge can be taught,

but wisdom must be learned

through experience.

~

*All there is to know is within you. You just have to open your heart to hear.*

*Regardless of what the eye sees or mind understands, the heart must feel and understand it, too. Spirit do not use language as we do; but thought. Their purpose is your purpose, their desire, your desire. Keep in tune with yourself and your Higher Self and all will be well.*

*Be clear in the heart and you will be clear in the head. Idealise when practical, otherwise just get moving and do those things that are necessary. This will help in reaching your destination.*

*Behold the sun, how dutifully it shines each and every day. But sometimes it is hidden behind the clouds; though it still shines it is as though it is no more. Be strong in your convictions that love and truth, like the sun, always shine, are always there.*

*Keep the clouds away.*

*. . . a spirit guide*

~

whatever happened to

Critical Mass?

Your exuberance

was well-founded then.

~

*When a soul starts out on its journey it is full of promise, eager, anticipating all the adventures yet to come. At first it is not disappointed, life unfolds as it would wish. But as it evolves, it comes into contact more and more with choice, which will mean activating freewill. Once that happens, all kinds of unpremeditated events occur and the soul becomes involved in the tug-of-war known as Cause and Effect. This is all necessary for the soul and for its evolvement.*

*Wisdom comes from the right use of knowledge. Knowledge alone is not enough, it is the wise application of it that is essential, and that is applied through the understanding and learning to give unselfishly of Love. Only when the soul has recognised and taken to itself the pure essence of Love can it really become wise, for then all things are understood perfectly. All things are loved. There is no bias, prejudice, judgement, only complete acceptance in the strongest possible way of the heart.*

*. . . a Messenger*

~

Look no further than the shining

cloud that floats above

in an endless harmony

with itself,

drifting with the wind

to atmospheric harmonies

~

*The mind plays tricks and cajoles us to believe we are only what it tells us to believe, whereas in fact we are always more. Our expansiveness is the new country to explore.*

*Imagining our true selves will become the new teaching, the new understanding of how we fit into the universe. For the universe is our Mother, able to create us and be a creator with us. If we reach out to any other part of Her creation in love, then we can attune ourselves to all that is available in mystery, in nature, and earthly and unearthly things. You are connected. Always and all ways.*

*It is the imagined idea of separation that has caused all the ills of the world. The story of Adam and Eve's ejection from the Garden is symbolic of your mind set. No longer need you be separate.*

*. . . Pierre*

~

Love one another,

No matter what!

~

*Love is not for the faint-hearted. It pushes buttons that may have grown rusty with age; it turns life upside down and in all different directions at once.*

*And what do we do? We fall headlong into it.*

*This is how God's love for us can make us feel.*

*Falling headlong into ecstasy.*

*. . . Pierre*

~

*When you look within your soul you find deep truths, deep truths that you thought you'd lost forever.*

*Imagine this, a shoreline that is forever changing. Over the aeons it moves backwards and forwards on a whim that is driven by changes to the planet. In essence, the fabric of the shore is still there, broken up into small pieces. Sand that was once rock, through a change and a turn of events, becomes solidified once more. Heat and impact fuse the grains. The shore is changed.*

*So, using that as an analogy, your soul must know what it is to be sand after being rock, returning then to what it once knew and identified with and truly was, but now with the experience that change has brought.*

~

Peace is always with you.

Just welcome it in.

It is shy.

It needs encouragement.

~

*The mystery that is life: ever unfolding its secrets, taken from the first word.*

*Light has shone through the universe. Then, trapped in miniscule capsules of what it has to offer, it is held so that life may begin infusing tiny particles, atoms, molecules, energy, until all coalesce, become animate – vibrating to a frequency beyond your understanding, but nevertheless real.*

~

Magic is a form of energy that exists

on a natural outpouring

of a soul's request that is sincere

and unselfish

and is heard throughout the cosmos.

And the cosmos cannot but help

answer the call.

~

*People need to be educated away from fear, cultivated away from the product of their past and shown that which, at present, is beyond their knowledge to understand.*

*Think of your own scientists. How many of them see the true outcome of their desire to be One among many? When the ego is softened and rounded at the edges then true values are shown, and humanity reaches its ultimate destiny while on this planet.*

*Let go of misunderstandings, let go of fears of what might be. Instead relish the present possibilities and know in your heart what is true for you – even if it differs from another.*

*. . . Adieu, Pierre*

~

How do we view ourselves;

the things around us?

If we look carefully, we can see

the condition of ourselves

by the condition of our lives.

~

*Sometimes there is nothing to be said. Other times, a hint or two of advice is timely. Each day, each hour has its own resonance and holds within it the power of the moment. Choose a moment and sense that power.*

*It is not a power that coerces or pushes this way or that, to do or not to do, it is a silent power of thought, deep thought, universal thought.*

*That moment that you choose, that quiet moment, is one of awareness, and with that awareness a connection is made with the universe – a universe that hears your every thought, mind to eternal mind, and knows you.*

~

Essence, Source, Wisdom, Love.

These are the substance of your true selves.

If you learn to truly understand the first two, you cannot fail to be rewarded with the last two.

~

*A great Light shines on the earth.*

*In secret places there are chasms and caverns and rocky places that hold Eternal Light. Places that no mortal person can enter, the Light too powerful, its strength necessary for what has been done to the earth.*

*... a Messenger*

~

Love gives

and never takes away.

Love is the song in the wind

That echoes

our heart's desire.

~

*We may see beauty in everything if we wish – a sunny day, a bird soaring, a sunrise, a sunset. There is ample opportunity for us to see evidence of beauty. And where does this beauty come from? Is it extant to us, or is it our inner response, our individual response that makes it beautiful? It is true, so many of us see beauty differently, so what makes the difference?*

*If we see beauty differently then we must, of course, see other things differently. But does this make us less a being of God? When we look around the universe and out to the planets, stars, nebulae, is it not obvious that all is different from its neighbour? The laws of the cosmos are like those of earth – they allow for infinite variety. So then let us embrace the infinite variety we have here, knowing it is all good, or comes from an original good. Perhaps if we see it as original good, it will be understood to be so, and in time may even be so by our own efforts of thought.*

*Seek not to see the differences as being bad or wrong, but rather part of the infinite pattern that enables us to be unique and yet part of a whole. We do not need to be the same to toe the line, to be like others, to be loved by God. He loves us no matter what we are. God admires us for what we seek to be in that scheme of things which supports a healthy, heavenly body for us all.*

*. . . Pierre*

*

# PART TWO

# PERSONAL JOTTINGS

*Reflections and memories*

Irresistibly, I look skywards whenever the sun goes down and the moon comes up. Is there some magnetism that draws my attention to the night sky and those tiny specks of light in their vault of black velvet? Are they similarly intrigued with my, or even *our,* existence and, if so, is it because we all have some deep link of commitment to each other?

And then I find myself travelling off into the wide black yonder to light and eternal sunshine, seeing pictures of pastel, watercolour landscapes, happy people and peaceful surroundings.

I have been taught that the astral plane is just the first of many stepping stones to other planes, so maybe the stars are symbolically a stepping stone; a way-station. Reaching the stars brings us to the borders of what we know in the Now, but once there we may find ourselves confronted with the possibility of infinite exploration. Maybe the word "astral" could also read "a place from which to view, assess, and move on".

~

Whilst dreaming/astral travelling, I must admit that I do have the tendency to believe that I am walking on what seems like solid ground rather than star dust, though at the same time there is an elemental feeling of space and other worlds that filters tantalisingly into my mind and won't go away. Am I really still connected to the earth, or am I floating free? I know, of course, that I am at the end of a fishing line and that, at any moment, I can be reeled in.

Regardless of that fact, I enjoy my forays into another type of existence, which for a while I used to fantasise as only "dream space" until I found that I could go back to exactly the same landscapes, the same people, time and time again, and pick up conversations that had been allowed to hang in the air till I returned.

I had once imagined that the world of spirit hung veil-like in the ethers just above my physical existence. I knew there were other existences that I couldn't see, although in my subconscious they were very, very real. They did not, however, seem necessarily accessible.

I now understand that there are dimensions beyond ours which in and of themselves are very tangible *and* real. These dimensions can be out there in space and just as easily right here in and around us at the same time. I often wonder if we could, in fact, be the equivalent of a veil-like existence for others.

~

The inherent goodness of being humanly kind is in us all.

Reading about the two homeless men who ran to help the victims of the Manchester bombing with little or no consideration of danger to themselves, was truly a heart-warming moment for me, and I suspect for others too. What added to that in multiples was the concerted support of those who recognised how they, in practical ways, could help these two men to change their fortunes in life by raising funds to help one find a life off the streets, and the other a property to call home.

~

I've come across a recipe for orange almond cookies. I haven't made them yet. They sound delicious, but I hesitate. How many times do I put off doing some baking because the temptation to devour the results in one go turns out to be too strong?

But these are biscuits, so there's just a chance they can be put in a tin and left for another day.

I don't think this is a spiritual analogy for my life. Is it?

~

The gifts of the soil are indeed wonderful, and we appreciate them for what they are – the food that keeps us alive – in the knowledge that all that is created for us comes from a Universal Consciousness that knows every bit of who we are, and knows how to look after us.

~

People are funny aren't they? They might come to your home and discreetly browse its contents, their thoughts sometimes unwittingly broadcasting how they would re-arrange things if it were their home. 'Why is *that* picture on *that* wall?' they might think.

But if it is not their home, it *is* the home of someone who is reflecting who they are and what in life gives them joy; how their belongings bring into their home a feeling of comfort and of gladness so that when they walk through their front door they feel welcomed by it all. This feeling changes when they change, when they wake up one morning and find that what they once loved no longer brings them joy.

I understand how it can be with our lives, that when we have reached a point that says: 'I am done with that, let's move on', everything wants to be different, re-organised, because *we* have moved on. When this happens to me I get the feeling it is time to re-decorate, change my colour schemes, take down the old and replace it with the new. Or even to reach for that spiritual book on the shelves of a bookshop that suddenly calls to me and says: 'This is the next step'.

When this happens I suspect that inside of myself things have changed, that I am different, have changed, however subtly. How many times have you heard someone say: 'Oh, I cleared out my wardrobe the other day and got rid of things I don't wear any more, and how free-ing it feels!'

I once helped a friend do this because she had said every time she opened her wardrobe she felt mentally exhausted. We filled a large number of bags, and had a good laugh while doing it.

If we are tempted to look at someone's home and have the very human urge to put our own identity on it, perhaps it is time to pause and consider whose home it is and what life is all about for them. We can spare a moment for those who struggle all their lives with the need to hold onto things; holding onto what no longer serves them but is, for them, impossible to do without. These "things" may be tangibly a part of them.

Could there be an underlying fear of what might happen if they were to let go of their possessions? This could change things, make life different, make life scarily unknown – leaving space, where before there was comforting clutter. By removing possessions, discarding them from their lives forever and changing the look and feel of their home might be a step too far, because it might also be a step that could change *them*.

Do we collect and hold onto things because they have become so much a part of us that we can no longer be ourselves if we remove them, or the "selves" that we think we are when it is possible our "selves" want to be free, to move on, want to grow into the promise that we were born with?

Those who have become hermits in their mound of unused, neglected, but impossible lives, live amongst years of belongings and the memories that have come with them. Sometimes, they can't get rid of them on their own; it is impossible for them. Life may have ground them into a hole they can see no way out of, and yet, given the chance, their spirit would want to fly free out of that hole.

If you know someone like this who is desperate for help but you do not know how to help them, if nothing else send out a prayer for the right help to be there for them at the right time. Thought can impress the ethers to enable this to happen. A bright, helpful thought for the good of another person is a strong and powerful tool to allow good things to come about.

The universe is full of thought, for this is how creation happens. Just by kind thought we can create a beautiful and positive outcome that will reach someone who is in desperate need.

~

Have you ever been in the situation where you are sharing something with somebody, and what you are sharing you know to be true, and they respond by looking at you as if you suddenly have two heads and are a being from another planet and they haven't a clue what you are on about? They think you are making up stories when really you are not. Is that because what you are telling them is not their truth? It is discombobulating to say the least.

So what is it that some of us understand when we listen to each other and what the other person is saying, but at other times we do not, or cannot? What is it that makes us at times aliens to each other, when really we are not? Do our brains work on crosswires that are only intermittently able to touch base with the other person; where we can only for a brief moment be aligned? Or are we just being individuals with a need to seek our own truth and not copy someone else's? It is something that makes me wonder where we exist in our own individual worlds, and where others exist in theirs.

～

When I take the bus and someone pulls out from their pocket or bag their mobile phone to answer a call and shares their conversation with the other passengers, I take out my hearing aids and sit back and enjoy the passing view beyond the bus window, and think that sometimes having a hearing loss is a blessing.

～

I once had the privilege of visiting an elderly lady who lived in a small hamlet in Victoria, south eastern Australia.

When her husband returned home after the First World War, he wanted to build a home he and his wife could call their own. Wood was scarce and came at a premium, but packing cases and fruit and vegetable crates were easily available.

The make-do house was meant to be a temporary home until they could afford to build something better. But the better home was never built because they came to love their packing-case house.

There were no doors separating one room from another, only curtains draped across each space. But this lady and her husband had raised a family in that small, humble home. I found it to be the most truly amazing place, and my visit made me realise that when love is built into a home and takes up residence, it is not easy to change that for something else.

How certain can you be that a new house will feel the same?

~

My soul sings with joy every morning as the sun comes up and lightens the day. Though dark clouds may gather, we all know the sky above is constantly blue and bright.

~

I want to find you, God, in today. As I say that, tears threaten to well up as if I've touched a forgotten chord.

I am on the 377 bus to Yeovil, and I've escaped Glastonbury for the day. I have a car, but somehow getting on the bus is an opportunity denied to car journeyers, the view through the bus window savoured at leisure, my timing and schedule according only to bus timetables and schedules.

The bus is picking up more passengers. This makes three stops so far and we've only just reached Street. A leisurely day indeed, and I am living it on a whim!

I have no idea what I will do when I get to Yeovil, and it doesn't matter. I will probably pay a visit to the old church, sit for a while, contemplate, and take in my surroundings until I feel the need to move on.

This is so different from my previous working life. Then, I dashed around, clock-watched, stumbled through life.

~

The buzz of the small café hums with shared words. The smell of coffee permeates those words with increasing gusto, and I wonder briefly if, as sometimes happens to me, some of these conversations are with strangers, where a few words of greeting turn into moments where we seem comfortable sharing our day with someone we may never meet again.

In a snapshot of time, a miniscule cameo of a stranger's life might be revealed in the retelling of what happened for them yesterday, or the day before.

I am witness to the weekly comings and goings of ordinary folk who have come to drink coffee in a small intimate café, and share what they have to give.

~

Memories are containers of ideas and aspirations. They build a picture of our life as it was back then; how we were back then. The good memories will need time to mull over, to savour as you would a good meal or a good wine, or a good whisky – a mental celebration of what has been treasured long enough to prove itself a valuable reminder of how wonderful life can be.

Bad memories need to be shovelled up and taken to the mental equivalent of a tip/rubbish dump/recycle centre, where they can be broken down, recycled, or destroyed. Recycled, yes! For some bad memories stay with us because they are the signposts that say: 'Do not go down that road again'.

~

I am in the supermarket, having a coffee, filling in time as my car has its occasional valeting.

At the car wash I am greeted with genuinely warm smiles and I know my morning has got off to a good start – not only a clean car, but lovely people cleaning it for me. I know some will say it's because, as a customer, they are grateful for my money, but I can't help feeling that this isn't always the case. That morning, I left wanting to share the smiles I had received. And I did!

How different the world would be if every single person on the planet shared a smile.

~

I am having egg and chips in the café.

Soul food for a middling, muddling Wednesday.

~

Being a writer brings you to a place that is a haven from the outside world. Poets have always known this. Authors of fiction are also aware of this – as well as the shrinking distance between them and their characters as they write.

However, there have been many occasions when I have wanted to type something and the words just won't come. It is frustrating, but then I go into the garden or drive to my allotment and get busy.

Busy-ness is a wonderful antidote to any lacklustre feeling of not being able to jump off the sofa or turn off the TV. I know that sounds mad, but opening the front door and actually stepping outside can often awaken my slothful body to a sense of freedom. My mind begins to think of alternatives to the day, when a moment before I might have been finding it hard to breathe without thinking how dreary life was.

I take a deep breath, no longer enveloped in the energy of "not doing", feeling instead the potential to be alive in activity and creativity.

Conversely, there are moments when I need a moment or two, or more, to stop and just "be" (as they say); where I want to be in touch with my every thought, feeling and desire; where I decide not to be tempted away to the "doing" – even if it means leaving the dishes in the sink and the laundry for another day.

This meditative process of inward contemplation can turn a dull Tuesday into a contemplative place where anything feels possible.

~

I have dark circles under my eyes and I want to do something about them. I have lived with them too long. Long enough!

The beautician looks at me in a caring, objective way, but I know I'm going to be her toughest assignment yet.

~

Supermarkets are hilarious. I always walk out with more than I'd needed, only to get home to find I've forgotten the milk – which is why I went there in the first place.

I have done this many times!

~

In my late forties I became a university student at La Trobe University in Melbourne, Victoria. I had to sit an entrance exam in Logic and, much to my surprise, I passed!

The Agora café was where students congregated, and it was where I met a Greek lady and we got chatting. She was in her early forties and was studying Psychology and Sociology. She hoped, eventually, to become a social worker.

My admiration for her was two-fold: she was doing a degree course in a second language, and she was also attending classes and writing assignments without her husband's knowledge. She said he would not have approved.

Her story was a salutary reminder about the true grit of women who, against all odds, find a way to fulfil their dreams.

~

I am old. No, redo that: I am elderly. How did that happen? Did someone overnight draw lines on my face so I could age ten years in a day?

In the wrong light, these lines are deeply etched, but they are an unveiling of a deeper self that has the benefit of years of life experience. So perhaps I can be proud of them?

~

The barista, or should she be baristess(?), at Canterbury's Waitrose is swirling the foam over my coffee in a practised way that has me momentarily mesmerised. Is it going to be a heart this time, I wonder? When she has finished we are both surprised. It is not a heart; it is an angel blowing a trumpet.

'You've made an angel with a trumpet!' I say.
She looks and laughs.
'How did you do that?'
'I don't know. It just happened.'

The angel is still there, still blowing her trumpet, until the very last sip.

~

The visions experienced during meditation are wonderful; they are our ticket to a promised land where all feels familiar and safe, even though we might find ourselves experiencing something new.

The meditation that I was taught many decades ago has given me the opportunity to reach out and discover the universe, to discover insights and knowledge that were often far removed from my own human perspective, experiences and understanding. But to learn how to do this, I first had to learn how to discipline my mind.

My mind has a tendency to wander, so my first learning curve was how to focus on one idea, or one image. I sat with others in a darkened room with a candle lit in the centre. We sat for sometimes two hours without moving, often at first not "seeing" anything as we tried to still our minds. Eventually I began to experience the true inner vision that can come with deep meditation.

Many times I saw visions of things that puzzled me – pictures and ideas that came from no former, or formal, knowledge. Years later I was able to find confirmation of what my meditations had been showing me, either through serendipitous moments of a book opening up at the right page, or buying a spiritual book that had fallen off a shelf and into my hands, or even hearing another person recounting their own meditations. There is great reward in finding your own visions confirmed in such a way.

~

London, Victoria: Winter, 2014

Beaty music blends with chatter behind the bar, at the tables and out through to the street. The blaring music fades into the background, the punchy words of the song passing only momentarily through the passage of my mind. I remain incognito amongst a mêlée of customers as the pub's sound system belts out poetic phrases to crazy rhythms. I am in my own world, being private in a public place.

The bar lady who comes to clear my table has bright red hair and is friendly. She has been generous with my "small" glass of red wine, which is larger than my usual small glass of wine at home. I drink it slowly, feeling mellow and content.

This pub interlude is because I am waiting for my connection to Canterbury. It is more bearable being in the pub than amongst the pigeons in the coach station opposite. They do their bit, though, hoovering up the crumbs of human untidy-ness.

(A passing thought: are the crumbs all they live on?)

The tables in the pub are close together, but privacy is assured by the pub's beaty music. My toes tip-tap spontaneously to jazz.

I am seventy-four years old, and life is wonderful.

~

Mexico City, August, 1993.

The impulse to go to Mexico had been strong. I imagined it would be the holiday of a lifetime. What it turned out to be was a learning tool for trust and faith.

I was on my way back to Mexico from a challenging two-day trip to Guatemala. The owner of the café on the Mexican side of the border was waiting for me as the bus pulled in at the border checkpoint.

A soldier with a rifle slung over his shoulder blocked the doorway of the bus and held out a hand for my passport, and I had the sudden uncomfortable feeling he wasn't going to give it back. But Maria was too quick, and before the soldier knew what was happening she had grabbed my passport and my hand, and we were walking briskly back to her café by the river.

We hugged each other warmly, gratitude pouring out of me. But then Maria began apologising. 'I am sorry,' she said, 'but the boatman needs to be paid a lot of money. He has been waiting for you.' He had been waiting four hours for me, so I understood how he might feel. I handed over all the money I had.

The students sitting in the boat had also been waiting and weren't happy, but on first sight of my grey hair and weary face, they relented and we became best buddies as I listened to them telling me about their travels. They came from different backgrounds: Belgian, French, Italian, Dutch, and were all fluent in Spanish – which was a great help at the checkpoint on the river when the guard said there was a problem with my visa and I knew there wasn't.

One of the students stood close to me, and I felt his protection. The other students chatted to the guards in their easy Spanish as if they were old mates, making jokes, lifting the mood of the moment. Through instinct, they knew how to handle the situation, and I realised I had once again been blessed with guardian angels.

There were many special and beautiful moments in my Mexican adventure, and some moments which weren't so special; moments where I found myself having to confront a fear that stubbornly resisted all my efforts to deny it. In the end I accepted the fear and just kept going.

*Yes, Louise Hay, you are right!*

I fell in love with Mexico, and the Mexicans. Despite the bumpy rides in buses over rocky roads, despite the moments when I felt uncertain about my reasons for being there and wishing I was home, I have never since regretted one minute of that inspiring journey.

But I still wanted to kiss the tarmac when I stepped off the plane at Heathrow Airport!

~

It's part of the pattern of life, and I am in the thick of it. Events come and go and move me into pockets of discomfort, pulling me in and spitting me out. All these events conspire to tell me something about myself, how I shape my own world, my life, my universe.

When depression hits, it fills our every cell. Every nuance of who we are is coated with the greyness of it. We try to plan a way out of it, but often you have to live through it and hope to reach the other side.

~

I have been reading a White Eagle book about the realisation of the Christ within, and it has stirred within me the question of where I have come to (reached) on my own path of searching for spiritual reality. Not so much knowledge, for that feels more like a teaching way to come to realisation rather than a feeling of my way towards understanding the reality of all that is good in God-consciousness; all that is freely available to us and is our reality if only we could see it and know it with certainty.

I am probably not explaining this very well, but the only analogy I can find to seeking the reality is that some see only the dark cloud above, whereas others choose to see the glorious sun that edges the cloud in golden light.

Seeing and understanding the truth of what is presented to us each and every day in our lives is a true blessing, guiding us to understanding what the creative impulse of the universe is aching to share. So I ask that you look at every moment you experience as if it is a God-given moment, full of potential wisdom that is showing you the reality of the spiritual life before you.

~

I have a bump on my head, and now a black eye. As if I needed that at my age!

It was all my own fault of course. Too much haste, too little regard for the things that stood in my way – like the garden rake hanging on the shed wall.

What was the lesson for me?

The answer was immediate: To pay attention and not assume that the way will always be made safe for me. In other words, to be responsible. Sensible!

Huh!

~

Revelation!

When it comes, it bursts through the wall of confusion like a bullet hitting its target. And it is free-ing. Any former anguish or pain is fittingly blown away, dissolved into forgiveness. A new dawn awaits and paces, counting the seconds until we move into action. And then each moment feels different from the past as a new awareness drives us forward.

No more contemplation. Now, all is action!

Contemplation of a different kind:

# ABOUT THE AUTHOR

Ann grew up in south east London in the 1940s and 50s. In 1971, she emigrated with her family to Melbourne, Australia, returning to England twenty-one years later to put down roots in a small country town in Somerset. She views her life as a continuing learning process, with an ever-growing awareness of the miracle of creation.

Writings include travel journals, poems, novels, articles for magazines and a collection of channelled messages. Hobbies include gardening, walking in nature, and reading a wide range of fiction and non-fiction.

Channelled messages:

*Wisdom from the Stars: An intergalactic dialogue with starseed and interdimensional beings. (Illustrated)* Previously published, without illustrations, entitled: "How Love Works" (now out of print).

*Raising Consciousness – Preparing for Change, Part One: Extraterrestrial Guidance for a Better Future.* (Co-authored with Elaine J. Thompson.)

Novels:

*The Celestial Ambulance: Life and work after death.* Ben tries to find his "feet" in the afterlife.

*Heather on the Hill:* Three lives entwined, a karmic debt repaid. A love story.

Printed in Poland
by Amazon Fulfillment
Poland Sp. z o.o., Wrocław

88975455R00060